Animal Habitats

The Penguin in the Snow

Text and Photographs by
Doug Allan

Oxford Scientific Films

Gareth Stevens Publishing
Milwaukee

Contents

Note: The use of a capital letter for a penguin's name means that it is a specific *type* (or *species*) of penguin (such as the Macaroni Penguin). The use of a lower case, or small, letter for a penguin's name means that it is a member of the larger *group* of penguins.

These Jackass Penguins are on a sandy beach in the tropics.

Adelie Penguins walk over the frozen sea.

Where penguins live

Penguins are sea birds which are unable to fly. Instead, they have become highly adapted for life at sea. Some travel far from land, making long sea voyages of four to five months and staying afloat through the roughest storms. Others stay closer to the shore, returning to the beach and their nests each night.

There are 18 different *species* of penguin in the world, and they are only found south of the *equator*, usually in places rarely visited by people. Some live in cool climates: around the shores of New Zealand or off the coasts of southern Australia or South Africa. Some live in the tropics: Jackass Penguins are found on the west coast of South America, and Galapagos Penguins inhabit (not surprisingly) the Galapagos Islands in the Pacific.

But penguins don't really like hot conditions; they can only manage in warm places because the sea is cool rather than warm. When they come ashore, they stand in the shade or nest under thick vegetation to stay out of the sun. They are really much more comfortable in cold climates, and it is in the far south that penguins are most numerous, down in the cold polar seas around Antarctica.

Penguins in Antarctica

Penguins are sociable animals. When at sea, they swim around in groups. They keep together by calling to each other. This not only helps them find food, but also guards against *predators*, which could more easily surprise and kill solitary individuals. When penguins come ashore, as they must do to breed, they gather in colonies known as "*rookeries*," where thousands or even millions of them nest close together. Penguins breeding on the coast of Antarctica or on the southern offshore islands have to cope with very cold conditions. Their rookeries are often found on bare, frozen ground or snow, and even during summer they can be faced with blizzards.

Emperor Penguins gather at their rookery. The cliffs in the background are made of pure ice.

When the sea ice breaks up in summer, these Adelies must climb over big lumps of ice to come ashore.

But during the summer, at least, the polar seas are almost free of ice. The waters are "open," and the penguins can swim and catch food close to their rookeries. When winter comes, however, the lower temperatures cause even the sea to freeze, until it becomes covered with a layer of ice up to 6 ft (1.75 m) thick. Like all birds, penguins breathe air, and since they cannot swim far under the solid ice, they have to *migrate* north for the winter. They travel as far as 500 miles (800 km) from their rookeries, staying in the open water where they can feed. Only when the ice breaks up again in spring do they return to the rookeries for another breeding cycle.

Penguins' lives are, therefore, divided between the sea and the land. They go to sea to catch their food, and they have to return to their rookeries on land for breeding. There are hardships to be faced in these two *environments*—from the weather and from predators. But, as we shall see, penguins are well adapted to survive in both environments.

5

Polar penguins and their rookeries

When the early explorers sailed into the unmapped south polar seas, they often warned the lookout to be alert and not only to search with his eyes for undiscovered islands, but also to use his nose. This is because in summer, at the height of the breeding season, you can often smell a penguin rookery long before you can see it! An offshore wind carries the smell of their *guano* well out to sea.

Close to the colony, the water seems alive with penguins, diving and calling as they swim back and forth, or standing on small icebergs and *floes* bobbing in the water. Sometimes, the lumps of ice are tightly packed together, with only narrow channels for the penguins to swim between. It may even be easier for them to walk on the ice than stay in the water.

Penguins must be able to reach the sea easily from their breeding colony. They cannot have a rookery where steep cliffs make it difficult for the birds to go in and out of the water. Nor can they set up a rookery where the surf batters too strongly against the shore. The ideal spot is often a low rocky shore or gently sloping hillside, with a beach at its base so that penguins can easily reach the sea. From this beach they can also select pebbles for their nests.

At this rookery, the penguins can easily enter and leave the sea over the gently sloping rocks at the water's edge.

Adelie Penguins nest together in large colonies. This one is on Signy Island in the South Orkneys.

Good places are fairly rare along the bleak, barren, and icy coastlines of Antarctica. This lack of available space often lowers the total populations of penguins. The size of a rookery is also often limited by the permanent snowfields around its edges. Penguins occupy every possible nest site on the bare ground. But they cannot nest on the snow, so there is a limit to how many birds can breed in one place.

Where conditions are suitable, however, there can be over a million penguins in one rookery. They might stretch well over half a mile (3/4 km) back from the beach, with some nests over 300 ft (100 m) above sea level.

Within the colony, the nests are usually clustered in groups of a few dozen to a few hundred, spaced with two or three nests in every square yard (sq m). Penguins are very defensive of their nest territories, and they will peck at other birds as they hurry by. But there are routes through the rookery that are recognized and used by all the birds. Only in the final few yards of the journey to its nest does the penguin have to risk an attack from unfriendly neighbors.

You can see how the Adelie's flippers still have the same shape as a bird's wing.

The penguin's body

Penguins don't look like birds. In fact, it's only when you look closely at them that you can see that penguins are almost completely covered with feathers. They *evolved* from birds that probably looked like the auks and guillemots you can see today. Unlike penguins, these birds can still fly. But like penguins they also dive and use their short wings for swimming underwater. As penguins evolved, they lost the ability to fly, but they became better adapted to life in water.

Penguins are warm-blooded animals. This means that the temperature of their bodies remains the same no matter how cold it is in the water or on land. They have developed a thick waterproof *plumage* of short feathers that overlap like tiles on a roof. The ends of these feathers are oily, so water won't soak through them. Underneath, next to the penguin's skin, there is a dense layer of fluffier *down* feathering. This traps warm air from the animal's body in the same way that a woolly vest does for you. Penguins also have a layer of fat immediately under their skin, and this also prevents heat loss from their bodies. With the insulation from their feathers and fat, penguins can easily spend long periods in the cold water.

The wings of penguins have become strong *flippers*. They use their flippers for swimming in the water and for fighting or defending themselves on land. Flying birds have especially light bones to make it easier to fly. But penguins' bones are heavy, making them the correct weight for swimming and diving. Penguins' bodies are streamlined in shape, which allows them to move smoothly and easily through the water.

You may have noticed that penguins all have about the same pattern of black and white on their bodies, but they have different color schemes on their heads and necks. Their bodies are *camouflaged*, pale underneath with a dark color on their backs. This makes it harder for hunting seals to see them against the pale sky when the seals look up from below the water. And an enemy at the surface, looking downward for penguins, will find it difficult to make out their dark shapes against the deep blue of the sea.

The different head markings show up clearly in a walking penguin or in one swimming on the surface of the sea. Ashore, the colors make their breeding displays more noticeable to each other. At sea, their bright markings help the penguins stay together.

The Chinstrap (above), Macaroni (below), and King Penguins (below right) each have a distinctively colored head.

Gentoos are among the fastest of the penguin swimmers.

Movement in water and on land

You really have to visit an aquarium or zoo with a glass-sided tank to appreciate how well penguins can swim. Their flippers (the modified wings) are attached to strong muscles in their chests. As the flippers beat up and down, they push the penguin through the water almost as if it were flying. The feet and sturdy tail feathers are used like rudders on a boat. They flick up when the penguin wants to change direction. Penguins are like little torpedoes. They zoom through the water with streams of small air bubbles running off their feathers.

When they are traveling at sea, they move by "porpoising." They swim underwater but leap in and out (like a porpoise) briefly every 15 seconds or so to breathe. This can also confuse any seal which is chasing them. While porpoising, they reach a speed of 20 mph (35 kph).

During their winter journeys, penguins may swim hundreds of miles (km) away from their rookeries. They always find their way back at the start of the next summer, but how they do this is still a mystery. They seem to be aware of the time of day and of how the sun's position changes between dawn and sunset. This helps them swim in a fairly straight line across the open ocean, back to their rookeries to start their breeding cycle.

10

Several Adelies and one Chinstrap leap from the sea onto the ice near their rookery.

Penguins are often faced with little ice cliffs at the water's edge where they want to come ashore. They come in close for a look, then dive down and swim rapidly up to the surface again, gathering speed so that they shoot straight out of the water and land safely on top of the ice cliff.

Once ashore, if they have a long way to go over snow, they will often drop onto their bellies. In this position, they push themselves forward with their feet. They slide quite quickly across the snow like sleds. This movement is called "tobogganing."

Different penguins have different ways of walking. Some can travel over much rougher ground than others, and this affects the type of places they choose for their rookeries. Big penguins like Kings prefer flat, gently sloping sites. Smaller, agile kinds—like Chinstraps—can colonize more uneven ground. On steep or icy slopes, their strong toes and claws grip tightly, and the birds may even use their beaks as an extra point of balance. Penguins also use their flippers to help them balance as they waddle along on land.

Emperors travel long distances over the frozen sea, so they often move by "tobogganing."

11

Feeding

Penguins do all their feeding at sea. In polar waters, the most abundant food is "*krill*," an animal about 2-3 inches (5-8 cm) long that looks like a shrimp. It lives in huge shoals (called "swarms") up to 10 miles (16 km) across in size, in which millions of tons of krill swim very close together. Penguins also catch fish and squid, which come close to the surface at night. But, when necessary, penguins can also dive deep in search of food. Adelies can swim down to over 200 ft (60 m) deep, while the Emperors go deepest of all, down to 800 ft (250 m).

The small Adelies and Chinstraps can stay underwater for up to five minutes. The larger Emperors can stay under even longer—up to 20 minutes. While a penguin is underwater, its heartbeat slows down, from about 85 beats per minute (a little faster than yours) to about 20 beats per minute. This means blood is pumped much more slowly around its body, so the oxygen supply lasts longer.

Adelies enter the sea to go on a feeding trip.

While this Gentoo is feeding its chick, you can see the fleshy, backward-pointing spines on the adult's tongue. These help the penguin grasp its slippery prey.

It is not yet known how the deep-diving Emperors catch their *prey* at these great depths. They have excellent eyesight underwater, but down there it is almost completely dark. Some scientists think they may be able to hear the sounds made by the animals they want to capture.

To make it easier to grasp and hold their slippery prey, the mouth and tongue of penguins are lined with fleshy, backward-pointing spines. Their stomachs are big in comparison to the size of their bodies. They can therefore eat a lot and feed far from home, but still have enough to give their chicks after swimming back.

Both the adult and the chick can eat food which looks much too big for them to swallow. Their beaks and throats can stretch to a surprising width, and a chick can sit happily digesting the head and front parts of a large fish with the tail still sticking out of its mouth!

It is hard to imagine just how much food is brought ashore to a big colony to feed all the chicks. In the South Orkney Islands, there are five million young Adelies in the middle of the summer. Someone figured out that you would need 70 big fishing boats working all the time to catch enough to feed those chicks. Yet adult penguins manage to do this every day.

This Chinstrap has its flippers spread to stay cool on a warm day.

Staying cool and keeping clean

Even in a world of snow and ice, a penguin's feather covering sometimes does too good a job for comfort. On calm, sunny days in summer, the birds can feel too warm. They may cool down by eating snow or drinking extra water. Or they fluff out their feathers so warm air from their skin can escape. They also open their mouths and pant—somewhat like a dog. If there is a slight breeze, they stand with their flippers stretched out and the feathers near their feet pulled up. When they do this, the flippers and feet act like radiators, giving off heat from the penguin's body.

To keep their feathers in good condition, penguins spend a lot of time washing and *preening*. In summer, the rookeries are very muddy places, and all the fighting and chasing make the penguins very dirty. When they go to sea to feed, before they swim away, they will often roll and splash in the shallows, rubbing themselves with their flippers to clean their feathers. When they return to the shore, they almost always spend a while preening on the beach. Like other water birds, penguins produce a special oil from a *gland* near the base of the tail. Using their beaks, they spread this oil onto their feathers. This helps keep the feathers waterproof and healthy.

A penguin cleans its feathers behind its flippers with its beak.

Every year, penguins completely replace their covering of feathers. It takes about 3-4 weeks for the old ones to drop out and the new ones to develop. During this period of *molting*, the penguins cannot go to sea and feed. Because they have to live off the fat they have stored in their bodies, they look scruffy and feel the cold more than usual. After the molt, however, their feathers are gleaming and healthy, and the penguins are ready to face the cold of the winter.

Penguins look somewhat scraggly when they are molting.

Male Chinstrap Penguins display for their partners.

Courtship and mating

Penguins start to return to their rookeries in spring (October in Antarctica). The adult males usually arrive first. They often take the same nest site as in previous years, but they add to its size by bringing new pebbles—sometimes stolen from a neighbor's collection. The nests are fairly crude, really just bowls of small stones with possibly some moss dropped in for a little more comfort. The nests do prevent the eggs from rolling away, however, and they help keep the eggs above the level of the melt-water streams which run through the colony during summer.

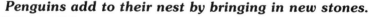

Penguins add to their nest by bringing in new stones.

Penguins often mate with the same partner each year. Although the pairs may have been separated over the winter, they recognize each other by their calls and the particular way they each behave during their "ecstatic" courtship displays. The male throws back his head until his beak points straight upward. He then slowly flaps his flippers to and fro, at the same time squawking loudly. In the large colonies, with breeding in full swing, the noise is deafening. It's as if each bird is trying to shout louder than the others.

Occasionally, two males will argue over a female or a nest site. They stand close together, each trying to stretch taller than the other, with breast feathers puffed out in a classic bullying pose. But this bluffing quickly turns into real fighting, when they lock their beaks together and beat each other wildly with their flippers. They do draw blood at times, but one bird usually turns and runs before serious injury is done.

When penguins mate, the female lies down on her belly and the male stands on her back, steadying himself with his beak and flippers. The male lowers his tail next to the female's, and mating takes place as *sperm* is passed from his body into her *cloaca*.

In the female's body, the eggshell forms around the *embryo*. This takes about eight days, and then the first of usually two eggs is laid. The second egg follows three or four days later.

Two Chinstraps fight over a nest site.

While this Adelie is standing up, you can see the broodpouch in which it incubates its eggs.

Incubation and hatching

Both parents become excited at the laying of the first egg. They take turns lying down on it, nudging it with their beaks and calling loudly to each other. They keep the egg warm—but not too warm, so the chick inside doesn't develop quite as fast as it could. It is only when the second egg is laid that they begin serious *incubation*. This means that, although the two eggs are laid three to four days apart, they hatch at nearly the same time.

It is usually the male who takes over the first spell of incubation, while the female goes to sea to feed. Laying takes lots of energy, and she must recover her strength.

Penguins have a bare patch of skin, called the *broodpouch*, on their bellies between their legs. This is normally hidden by a loose fold of feather-covered skin, but while they are incubating, the broodpouch is more exposed. So when the penguin settles on its eggs, it tucks them between its feet and this bare skin, with the feathery fold wrapped around them. The eggs don't touch the ground at all, but are kept safe and warm next to the parent's body.

Adelies incubate comfortably through an Antarctic blizzard. How many tails can you see sticking up through the snow

Keeping the egg warm is very important, for the developing chick will die if the egg cools too much. Even through the blizzards which can last for up to three days, the adults sit tight on their eggs. They let the snow pile up around them until only their beaks and tails are left sticking out. They may look cold, but their wonderful insulation of feathers and fat keeps them comfortable.

When one adult comes back from feeding at sea, it runs toward its nest, then calls to its partner. They go through a greeting display of head-waving and flipper-flapping, accompanied by loud squawking. When both are ready, one rises from the eggs to let the other take over. The parents never leave the eggs unattended, because of the presence of predators like Skuas, Sheathbills, or gulls. These birds are always on the lookout for unguarded eggs and will eat them if they have the chance.

Incubation usually lasts about 35 days. The parents know that hatching is due, because the chick inside often makes cheeping noises before actually breaking out of the egg. Hatching is hard work for the chick; it can take two days for it to break out completely. First it chips a small hole in the egg with its "egg tooth"—a special hard tip on its beak. Then it cracks right around the middle of the shell and uses its feet to push apart the halves. The parent doesn't help at all, but as soon as hatching is complete, it tucks the chick gently back into the broodpouch to keep it warm.

Hatching has just begun for this Adelie chick.

An Adelie chick seeks food by first pecking its parent's beak. It then feeds directly from the adult's mouth.

From hatching to fledging

Newly hatched penguin chicks rapidly become chilled when exposed to the snow or wind. So, for the first week of their lives, they mostly stay out of sight underneath their parents, showing themselves only when they want to be fed. Each chick makes high-pitched piping calls, which the parent recognizes. The adult bends its head over, and the youngster will stretch its neck up to peck at the underside of the parent's beak. After one or two repetitions of this act, the adult brings food back up into its mouth from its crop. The crop is a special storage sac in the penguin's throat for half-eaten food. The chick puts its own head right inside the parent's mouth to get this food for itself.

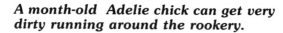

A month-old Adelie chick can get very dirty running around the rookery.

The krill, fish, or squid which the adults bring back is very rich, and the chicks grow rapidly. As they get bigger, so their appetites increase, and both parents need to go to sea to fetch enough food. While the chicks are alone, they gather in "*crèches*" or nursery groups. In groups like this, they can more easily stay warm, and they are also less likely to be killed by predatory birds. Some non-breeding adults also stay around, and they help protect the youngsters from attack.

The returning adult will feed only its own chick. When it has hatched two youngsters, it will often run away as the chicks approach, so they have to chase in order to be fed. This behavior ensures that if food is in short supply, it is the stronger, healthier chick who will get the food and so have the best chance of survival.

Many youngsters die during the crèching period. At this stage the chicks are too big to be sheltered by their parents, but their covering of down is sometimes not enough protection against spells of bitter weather.

About six weeks after hatching, the chicks begin to *fledge*. They lose their coat of fluffy down to reveal their proper feathering. They make their way down to the beach, standing on the edge of the surf with their necks stretched forward, as if wondering what to make of it all. Then, in a rush, they take to the water. The young penguins head straight out to sea. It will be two to four years before they return to the colonies to start their own breeding.

These Adelie chicks have only to lose the tufts of down on their heads. Then they will be fully fledged.

Emperor Penguins don't build nests. The males keep their eggs up off the ice on their feet for all the incubation, which lasts through the Antarctic winter darkness.

The family life of Emperor Penguins

Emperors are the largest penguins, standing about 4 ft (1.2 m) tall and weighing around 70 lbs (30 kg). Compared to the smaller types of penguins which take only two months, it takes Emperor chicks four months from hatching before they are able to take care of themselves. The only way they can be ready to leave the rookery in the middle of summer is for the adults to begin their breeding cycle much earlier than other penguins.

The newly-hatched Emperor chick stays warm by remaining in the broodpouch, sitting on the parent's feet, and only occasionally looking out from behind the feathers.

The Emperors begin to gather at their colony sites in April, at the start of the Antarctic winter. They don't have their rookeries on land, but on the ice of the frozen sea. After finding their partner (again by recognizing each other's calls), they mate and the single egg is laid in May or early June. Almost as soon as it is laid, the female gives it to the male. He nudges it with his beak up onto his feet and into his broodpouch. Emperor Penguins build no nest, and the egg is kept up off the ice on the father's feet. Here it stays for the whole incubation. The female then sets off to areas where the sea is not frozen, and there she feeds. The male is left alone to look after the egg.

In Antarctica, it is dark all the time through the middle of the winter. The sun doesn't rise above the horizon, and it is extremely cold. The male Emperors stand quietly shoulder to shoulder in "huddles," staying warmer than if they quarrelled among themselves like the other kinds of penguins we have seen. They sometimes eat snow, but they have no solid food. During the two months of incubating, they live off the fat stored in their bodies and lose up to one-third of their body weight.

The females toboggan back just as the egg hatches, and it's now the males' turn to go and feed. All through the spring and early summer, the parents come and go with krill or squid for their chicks. As the ice on the sea breaks up, the journey from the colony to the feeding areas becomes shorter. This makes it easier to keep the chicks supplied with food.

In some years, the ice breaks back too far, into the rookery itself, and many chicks are lost when they are carried to sea on floes.

Fledging is in early January, so the young Emperors take to sea when food is most plentiful.

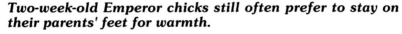

Two-week-old Emperor chicks still often prefer to stay on their parents' feet for warmth.

23

The Leopard Seal hunts penguins in the broken ice.

Enemies and defense

The main enemy of penguins at sea is the Leopard Seal. During summer, numbers of these seals gather near the rookeries, catching the penguins as they swim to and from their feeding areas. Leopard Seals have big front flippers, which enable them to turn quickly while they chase their prey underwater. Although penguins too can turn and dodge rapidly, they become tired more quickly than the seals. Often, the seals pursue them into fairly shallow water, where the surging waves and bubbles confuse the penguins even more.

Once it has caught a penguin in its powerful jaws, the Leopard Seal separates the skin from the carcass by biting off the tail and feet and beating the body against the surface of the sea. The skin, which the seal doesn't eat, is pecked over by Giant Petrels, fluttering Wilson's Petrels, and Pintado Petrels. These birds settle on the water in great numbers near a penguin kill. Young penguins going to sea for the first time are especially at risk, for they are less experienced and less aware of the danger, and they cannot swim as well as the adults.

Penguins are normally safe from predators ashore. Skuas or Giant Petrels only attack weak or wounded adults, since the healthy adults are much too good at defending themselves. They peck strongly with their sharp beaks, and a punch from their flippers is extremely painful.

This Brown Skua has stolen a penguin's egg from the rookery.

But it is a different story when they have eggs or chicks. Pairs of Skuas work together to distract the adult penguin away from its nest. They repeatedly fly or hover very low over the colony, or they parade in front of one particular nest. The penguin becomes annoyed and moves to try to peck at one Skua. This is when the other darts in to seize the egg or chick.

The Sheathbill has a very clever way of obtaining food for its young at the expense of the penguin. The bird watches until a penguin chick is being fed. It then flies in very quickly and pecks or flaps its wings against the head of the chick. In surprise and fright, the chick turns its head away, often dropping some food on the ground. The penguin chick doesn't pick it up, but the Sheathbill lands to collect it, to take back to its own chicks.

The Sheathbill grabs food as it is passed from the adult Adelie to its chick.

When scientists count penguins, they dab them with paint to make sure they don't count the same bird twice.

Penguins and people

In the early days of voyages to the south polar seas, it was always the penguins who came off worse in their meetings with people. Because the penguin rookeries were easy to reach by boat, explorers would land and take the penguins' eggs for their own food. They also killed many adults, both for eating and for the oils they could extract from their bodies.

This scientist is weighing a Chinstrap Penguin.

Nowadays, there is much more concern about the conservation of penguins. This means protecting the rookeries and trying to leave the penguins as undisturbed as possible. For example, when scientists want to study a rookery, they sometimes have to fly in by helicopter. They take care to land a safe distance from the penguins, so that the birds are not frightened off their nests by the noise.

By carefully counting the number of nests in the same colonies each year, scientists have discovered that some penguin populations are actually increasing. This could be because the whales (which also eat krill) have been greatly reduced in numbers by hunting. The penguins may be finding more food, more easily. This would allow them to raise more chicks, and so the population would expand.

Recently, however, people with special fishing boats have begun to catch the krill too, for eating by humans or farm animals. In Japan, you can buy "krill-cakes" just as here you can buy fish-cakes. It is now quite possible that people will take too much krill out of the sea, making it scarce for the penguins and all the other sea creatures that depend on it for food. Agreements have been signed between countries to limit the catches. But until we are more certain that it is not causing harm, it would be better if large amounts of krill were not harvested at all.

At the moment, there is not much threat of *pollution* where the polar penguins live. But oil and minerals have been discovered in the Antarctic, and if drilling begins, the danger of pollution could arise. If drilling does take place, it will be very important to have safety measures that prevent any spillage of oil. When oil gets onto the plumage, the feathers lose their waterproofing, and the penguin becomes chilled. If the birds swallow the oil, they can be poisoned.

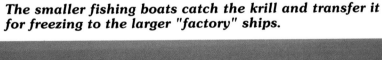

The smaller fishing boats catch the krill and transfer it for freezing to the larger "factory" ships.

A young Chinstrap chick approaches a Southern Fur Seal which is visiting the colony.

Friends and neighbors

Penguins in a rookery are so noisy, dirty, and quarrelsome that most other birds can't claim a space for nesting. Only the Sheathbills manage to find places under ledges of rock too low for the penguins to use. Around the edges of a colony, however, many kinds of birds may have their nest. The Giant Petrels are about the same size as a turkey. They like the tops of ridges, where the wind blows strongly and makes it easier for them to take off. At sunset, the tiny Wilson's Petrels fly back from the sea to their nest sites. Fluttering and swooping more like bats than birds, they make chirping noises to their mates so they can find their holes. On the cliff ledges overlooking the rookery, Pintado and Snow Petrels rear their chicks, and Blue-eyed Cormorants build their seaweed nests.

Seals haul themselves out on the same beaches as the penguins use. The huge Elephant Seals lie in groups of 20 or more while they go through their summer molt. Just as the penguins replace their feathers, so the Elephant Seals renew their fur. Weddell Seals, too, stretch out on the rocks.

Out at sea, the vast amounts of krill attract many different sea birds, seals, and whales. Out here there are also gulls, Terns, and Albatrosses, as well as the birds that live near the penguins on land.

Sometimes, different kinds of penguins nest together. Can you identify the Chinstraps, the Macaronis, and the Adelies?

The penguin's biggest neighbors are also the biggest animals in the world—the whales. Instead of having teeth, a whale that feeds on krill has many long strips of tough skin growing down from the roof of its mouth. These strips are called "baleen." As it swims steadily with its mouth open, the whale takes in huge amounts of water and krill. The krill is trapped on the rough edges of the baleen, but the water flows through the gaps. Then the great tongue pushes the krill down the whale's throat. It is quite amazing to think of these huge animals, up to 100 ft (30 m) long, feeding entirely on krill less than 3 inches (8 cm) in length.

This Weddell Seal has come ashore on the same beach that the penguins use.

29

Life in the snow

Many animals besides penguins eat the krill, squid, and fish. Leopard Seals, Skuas, and Giant Petrels can feed directly on these small animals, as well as on the penguins. At the rookery, Sheathbills and Skuas steal the penguins' eggs. We can show what eats what with a diagram called a food chain.

It may look as though penguins have many predators. In fact, the Skuas, Giant Petrels, and gulls only kill adult penguins which have been injured and are less able to defend themselves. They would probably die anyway. Similarly, it is the weak chicks that are killed—the ones chilled by blizzards or those who cannot chase fast enough after their parents for food.

Food chain

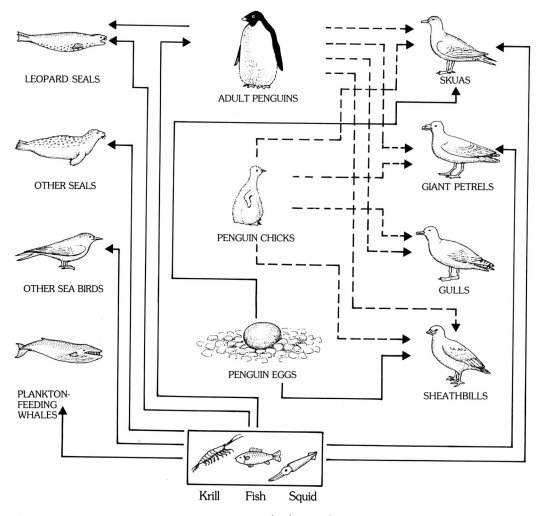

- - - - dead or weak penguins

These Adelie Penguins seem to be wondering which is the best way across the floes back to their rookery.

Penguins are wonderfully suited to life among the snow and ice, in the water, and on the land. They live a surprisingly long time for small animals. Adelies can be up to 12 years old, and Emperors can be over 20. The polar penguins are plentiful today. They live in a part of the world with no factories, no farming, and very few people. They have a very clean *habitat*, with hardly any pollution. But people are beginning to think about developing these areas for oil drilling and for krill fishing. It is important that they also remember the needs of the penguins, so they do not spoil the habitat for these tough little birds.

Emperors beginning to congregate under the high cliffs of Antarctica.

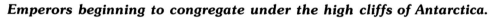

31

Glossary and Index

These new words about penguins appear in the text on the pages shown after each definition. Each new word first appears in the text in italics, just as it appears here.

Reading level analysis: SPACHE 3.6, FRY 5, FLESCH 89 (easy), RAYGOR 7, FOG 6.5, SMOG 5.7

Library of Congress Cataloging-in-Publication Data   Allan, Douglas. The penguin in the snow. (Animal habitats) Includes index.
Summary: Text and photographs depict penguins feeding, breeding, and defending themselves in their natural habitats.
1. Penguins–Juvenile literature. [1. Penguins] I. Turpin, Lorna, ill. II. Title. III. Series.
QL696.S473A43 1988b   598.4'41   87-9968   ISBN 1-55532-295-6   ISBN 1-55532-270-0 (lib. bdg.)

North American edition first published in 1988 by
Gareth Stevens, Inc.
7221 West Green Tree Road   Milwaukee, WI 53223, USA
Text copyright © 1988 by Oxford Scientific Films.

US Editor: Mark J. Sachner.   Series Editor: Jennifer Coldrey.   Line Drawings: Lorna Turpin.
Scientific Consultants: Gwynne Vevers and David Saintsing.

The publishers wish to thank the following for permission to reproduce copyright photographs: **Doug Allan** for front cover, title page, and back cover, pp. 3, 4, 5, 6, 7, 9 all, 10, 11 both, 12, 13, 14, 15 both, 16 both, 17, 18 both, 19, 20 all, 22 both, 23, 24, 25 both, 26 both, 28, 29 both, and 31 both. **Oxford Scientific Films Ltd**. for p. 2 (photographer David Curl); p. 8 (photographer Andrew Lister); p. 27 (photographer E.C.G. Lemon).